HOW TO GET EVEN WITH YOUR EX

MARSHA POSNER WILLIAMS

&

MIKE PRICE

Illustrated by Greg Tenorio

CCC Publications ● Los Angeles

Published by

CCC Publications
20306 Tau Place
Chatsworth, CA 91311

Manufactured in the United States of America

Cover design & illustrations © 1986 CCC Publications

ISBN: 0-918259-09-6

First CCC Publications printing — March 1987

If your local U.S. bookstore is out of stock, copies of this book may be obtained by mailing a check or money order for $3.95 per book (plus $1.00 to cover sales tax, postage, and handling) to: CCC Publications/20306 Tau Pl., Chatsworth, CA 91311.

PUBLISHER'S NOTE

It is a rare exception that a manuscript comes to a publisher that applies to every adult in the world. A book that anyone can relate to and everyone can understand. **This is such a book.**

You've all probably heard the old cliche, "There are only two sure things in life—death and taxes." Whoever said that was wrong. Some day, through some scientific breakthrough, we may live forever, and taxes could be abolished (may it happen in your lifetime!). I believe there is only **one** sure thing in life—**EXes**! Everybody either has or will have an EX (not just husband or wife). It's impossible to go through life without having some kind of an **EX.**

The purpose of this book is **not** to cause anybody harm. It is intended as a catharsis in that it gives you a way to release many of your stored up frustrations. Please feel free to fantasize in your mind the acting out of every way to get even. In other words, **don't** take all the suggestions literally. Sometimes it is just as therapeutic to pretend.

Fortunately for us all, the authors recognized a need for a fun approach to an oftimes painful subject. When you combine the wonderful writing talents of Marsha Posner Williams, 1986 Emmy Award winning Producer **("Best Comedy Series",** *The Golden Girls)* with popular Tennessee columnist and comedy Director, Mike Price, the results can only be deliciously funny. I am very grateful to have had the opportunity to publish their work. I hope you enjoy it as much as I did.

— Mark Chutick

P.S. I just remembered one more sure thing in life, I did it for the **money**! (My success will just kill **my** Exes—see, I'm already learning!)

CONTENTS

AUTHORS' NOTE

Before you enter the wonderful world of Getting Even With Your Ex, consider this: We, as your guides, have no way of knowing which sex your Ex (or Exes) happens to be.

Also, we have no way of knowing whether your Ex is a husband, wife, lover, boss, lawyer, doctor, etc., etc., etc.

Only you know that.

Now, the specific gender of the vict... er, subjects dealt with herein will, in certain limited cases, become obvious. For the most part, however, these valuable and satisfying suggestions are uniformly applicable to either, or both, or any—sex, that is.

So, in general reference to your particular Ex, do we dare simply use "him"? Nope. Too restrictive and misleading. Nor do we use "her," for the same reasons.

We look at it this way. An EX is an EX is an EX. That's it. That's the solution. And that's the word. In the final analysis, an Ex has no sex.

Certainly not with you.

And not with us, either. We're on **your** side.

INTRODUCTION

Look, we know you're basically a fine human being.

We know how hard you tried—**really** tried—to make it work. We also know what a rotten deal you got—the way things turned out. Furthermore, we know that if there's **any** justice in this world, you deserve to **get even.**

We want to help you.

You might say, "I want to get even, but I can't do the things you suggest. Some are underhanded and some are impossible." Well, we say to that, "You never know how much satisfaction you'll feel by getting even until you try." Remember, your EX was the instigator. . . it's **all** your EX's fault.

You don't need to be a fanatic about this. Just consider these tips, use your own judgement and follow your impulses.

WHY GET EVEN, YOU ASK?

Think back.

Think of all the **Little Things**. . .

Then think of all the **Medium-sized Things**, the ones you could have made a big deal out of, but you were just too damn nice a human being.

Then remember the **Big Things**, the really monumental indignities and insults and injustices you suffered.

And you're asking **us** why you should get even?

This Book is Dedicated To

Sue!

(Your EX's Name Here)

QUIC

Paste your Ex's photo over every picture in every local branch of the U.S. Post Office—then call 911.

Six minutes into your Ex's porno tapes, overdub with episodes of The Gospel Hour.

Donate all your Ex's organs to medical research. Now.

Blunt the tips of your Ex's earring studs.

Send a set of votive candles. . . made out of chicken fat.

KIES!

During a TV Telethon, call up and pledge $10,000 in your Ex's name. Hopefully, the station will flash your Ex's name and announce their generosity.

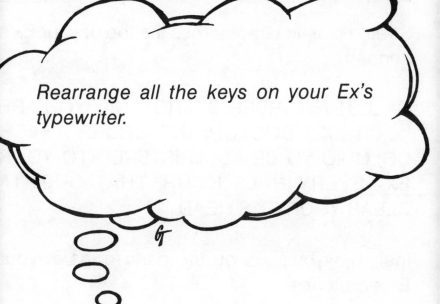

Rearrange all the keys on your Ex's typewriter.

HOSPITAL FUN

If you think your Ex is sick of you now, wait until they're in the hospital. Then. . .

PHONE THE FINANCE OFFICE, ANNOUNCE THAT YOU'RE WITH YOUR EX'S INSURANCE COMPANY AND THEY'VE BEEN CANCELLED.

Stretch plastic wrap across the top of your Ex's bedpan.

CALL THE NURSES' STATION, SAY YOU ARE YOUR EX'S DOCTOR AND ORDER A HIGH COLONIC TO BE ADMINISTERED TO YOUR EX—EVERY HALF HOUR. THAT OUGHTA CLEAR YOUR EX'S HEAD.

Install joy-buzzers on the hand-grips of your Ex's crutches.

3

TOILET TRAINING

Glue or tape a sign to the toilet seat in your Ex's house or apartment. Naturally, it should be imprinted on the underside (so it's clearly readable when lifted) with the following message:

ALIMONY PAYMENT DUE

That's for your Ex to read. This one's for your Ex's friends, neighbors, relatives and—most importantly—romantic companion's benefit:

DID OLD
(Your Ex's Name)
HAPPEN TO MENTION ANYTHING ABOUT THE HERPES?

EX-TRA, EX-TRA, READ ALL ABOUT IT

In terms of Getting Even With Your Ex, your local supermarket is more than merely a source of insect repellant. Look, over there by the door. . .

It's a Bulletin Board!

Believe us, bulletin boards are indeed a wonderful place to communicate with the public—which is also, remember, your Ex's public.

Undoubtedly, many of your Ex's friends and neighbors also shop at the same supermarket. Good. Here's a terrific way to help your Ex keep those all-important lines of communication open and maybe even develop a whole new set of impersonal relationships. And all it takes is a neatly printed 3x5 index card. . .

ENOUGH FUN IN YOUR SEX LIFE?
NOT TO WORRY—ONE CALL STOPS IT ALL!
(Your Ex's Name & Phone Number Here)

OR...

FOR SALE
(Your Ex's Car, Make & Model)
$100. or Best Offer
(Your Ex's Phone Number)

Won't your EX love all those annoying calls!

ONCE MORE WITH FEELING

Music, they say, soothes the savage beast. Or the other hand. . .

♫ RE-TUNE YOUR EX'S PIANO SO THAT NO MATTER WHICH KEYS ARE HIT THEY ALL PLAY THE SAME NOTE.

♫ SAW YOUR EX'S DRUMSTICKS ALMOST ALL THE WAY THROUGH.

♫ STASH A HUGE WAD OF PRE-CHEWED BUBBLEGUM IN THE BELL OF YOUR EX'S TRUMPET. Wah-wah-wah. . .

♫ SOAK YOUR EX'S CLARINET REED IN ALUM. Kissee-kissee!

♫ DRILL MICROSCOPIC HOLES IN YOUR EX'S TROMBONE. YOUR EX WILL GO CRAZY TRYING TO PLAY IN TUNE.

♪ SWITCH ALL THE COVERS ON YOUR EX'S ALBUMS, CASSETTES AND COMPACT DISCS.

And picture this: If you could only thread a piece of clear fishing line filament from the bass drum pedal to the top of your Ex's head. Guess who'd be nodding 'yes' all night long.

STICK IT TO 'EM

Here is a Cosmic Truth: The best vehicle in the worl
for Getting Even is your Ex's car.

And the easiest part of your Ex's car for Getting Eve
is the rear bumper.

And the best thing about the rear bumper of your Ex'
car is that, although he or she hardly ever sees i
everybody else does.

And thus there's no telling how much time can pas:
days or weeks or maybe even months, until your E
discovers that somebody has been engaged in
little automotive decorating. . .

Bumper Stickers. Getting Even-wise, they're a moder
miracle. Effective, long-lasting and thoroughly em
barrassing, bumper-stickers are a richly rewardin
means of informing the world at large just exact
what sort of person your Ex really is.

You can make your own bumper-stickers simply b
using pre-gummed paper, a felt tipped pen o
stencils.

Right now, for instance, let us deal with the fact th
your Ex was—and no doubt still is—a rather ur
imaginative lover. . .

GREETINGS!

Research has proven that many peopl
weaken when the Ex's birthday rolls around

Let it be known you still think of them.

Rip out the following. Neatness doesn't cour
Fold together and mail in a regular greetin
card envelope.

".. A thought... on your Birthday the happy were really I those of Best Years Life, your of"

← FOLD →

"You've lived way too long..."

TRANSIT EX-PRESS

🚌 Fix your Ex's gauge so it always reads full.

🚗 Enhance summer driving fun. Hide a couple of pounds of halibut in your Ex's trunk.

🚌 Speaking of fishing, a lot of people wonder where the best place is to store those big fat night crawler fishing worms. In your Ex's crash helmet sounds like a good place to us.

🚗 Does your Ex drive a motorcycle? This one's easy. Shorten the kickstand.

🚌 Grind a flat spot on just one wheel of your Ex's roller skates.

🚗 Set all the buttons on your Ex's car radio to a station you know your Ex really hates. And don't hesitate to keep doing it again and again and again. . .

AN EX-ORCISE IN GOOD FAITH

Is your Ex lonely on Sunday mornings? And the rest of the week? Maybe some truly sincere mail might brighten the day. You can be sure that they'll get plenty of it by sending one dollar (in your Ex's name, of course) to every television preacher and faith-healer on the tube.

In return for this modest outlay of cash, you can sleep soundly until noon—or until dark, if that's your thing—secure in the knowledge that your Ex will be swamped with relentless pleas for more and more and more cash. But then, that's your Ex's problem, isn't it?

AMEN.

VACATION TIME

The sun, the surf, the slopes... wherever they go, you should stay with them in spirit and memory. As a matter of fact, you can actually be of great help to your Ex even before the trip begins. Really. Think about it...

Sometimes they don't know where to go— despite all the times you told them. Here, then, are a few places you might helpfully and enthusiastically recommend to your Ex:

A SINGLES CRUISE INTO THE BERMUDA TRIANGLE

A SHOPPING TRIP IN DOWNTOWN BEIRUT

HANG GLIDING FROM MT. EVEREST

THE TANZANIAN TSE-TSE FLY FESTIVAL

A MOUNT ST. HELEN'S VOLCANO EXPEDITION WITH WHITE LAVA RAFTING

A FUN-FILLED NICARAGUAN HOLIDAY

THE SIBERIAN YAK ROPING RODEO

THE JOAN OF ARC FIRE-BATON TWIRLING TRIP TO EUROPE

THE "OPEN END TURKISH PRISON TOUR"

MORE QUICKIES

Stir some of those little multi-colored fish tank
rocks into your Ex's trail mix. Yummy, yummy.

TRAIN YOUR EX'S PET TO RELIEVE ITSELF
EVERY TIME THE PHONE RINGS.

Deposit a supply of pure, healthful honey into
the bottom of you-know-who's purse.

SIGN UP YOUR EX AS A VOLUNTEER WORKER
FOR EVERY POLITICAL CAMPAIGN—ON BOTH
SIDES.

EX-PLAIN YOURSELF

While he or she or it is out of town, have a silent security alarm system wired into your Ex's house. Whenever he or she or it finally returns home and opens the door, the alarm will immediately be activated... and within minutes, of course, the entire neighborhood will be surrounded by a S.W.A.T. team.

*There's no way to explain this one. All your Ex can expect to hear is, "Hey do you expect us to believe that some crook snuck in here and **installed** a burglar alarm?"*

Here's a greeting card that works. On any day
For any occasion.

Pucker up.

Baby.....

← FOLD →

"..This is the Kiss Off!"

COMING EX-TRACTIONS

Watch this. It's a beaut. The only thing you need is a needle-nosed pliers. That's one of these:

Now, slip into your Ex's closet and carefully remove a single tooth from near the bottom of every zipper in every garment.

Oh, sure, it'll zip closed alright. . . but it won't **stay** closed. No way. Trust us.

MORE IMPORTANT BULLETINS

Let's face it, one of you had to move out. In the stirring words of Henry VIII, "Living together does not a genuine Ex make." Good old Hank. Now there's a guy who really knew how to cut his losses.

Even if you were the one who found it necessary to relocate, that doesn't mean you have to abandon the neighborhood altogether. Drop in at the local supermarket and leave behind a truly meaningful memento, one which will continue to darken up your Ex's life long after you've packed your 'jammies and changed your address.

This trusty little 3x5 index card posted on the store's bulletin board is guaranteed to keep the memory of you fresh and colorful in your Ex's mind:

> ROOM TO LET — $25 A MONTH
> FREE BEER
> PARKING ON THE LAWN
> (Your Ex's address goes here, in BIG letters)

SAY IT WITH FLORALS

Nothing draws more attention (delivered at work or left on the doorstep) than the unexpected appearance of an elaborate floral wreath, especially when it is adorned with a sincere, meaningful message printed in BIG, FAT LETTERS... which are **easy-to-read-even-from-a-distance**, of course.

Consider how deeply touched your Ex will be, and how sharply observant your Ex's co-workers and neighbors will be, and how very interesting your Ex's explanation will be, whenever he or she is the designated recipient of...

Sometimes simpler is better:

This moving message is self-evident:

☺ **INSIDE JOKE** ☹

This is something that always works. Always.

Whatever you do, whatever your income, social status, race, religion, or station in life, it's a lifetime-guaranteed cinch. It's beautifully simple and you do it whenever and wherever you see your Ex.

You laugh.

That's all. Just start laughing. As the occasion demands:

a) chortle   f) snigger
b) chuckle   g) titter
c) giggle   h) guffaw
d) cackle   i) bray
e) snicker   j) all of the above

That's it. Just simply laugh. And not just a lightweight "tee-hee". Tee-hees are ho-hum. Get **down** with it. Remember, there are no wrong laughs. Not when you are the laugher and your Ex is the laughee.

EX-TEND AN INVITATION

Leave this note for the collectors to find on top of your Ex's trash:

Here's a bumper sticker to make sure your Ex
will have plenty of company at those gritty truck
stops. If your Ex even gets there.

**TRUCKERS ARE
GUTLESS PUNKS**

READ THE UN-EX-PECTED

Your Ex may have read all the magazines in their bathroom, but their friends haven't.

Go into your Ex's place and take the cover off one of the bathroom magazines, inserting a slick, hardcore magazine of the same size.

With any luck at all, your Ex's friends and relatives will have the bathroom experience of a lifetime.

EVEN MORE QUICKIES!

Call ahead and cancel all your Ex's vacation reservations.

PUT GARLIC OIL IN YOUR EX'S SHAMPOO.

Put popcorn kernels in your Ex's electric blanket

ENLIST YOUR EX IN THE GREEN BERET.

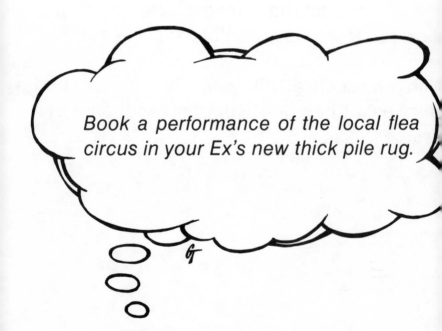

Book a performance of the local flea circus in your Ex's new thick pile rug.

GIVE YOUR EX AN ANTFARM. . .
WITH A SMALL HOLE IN THE GLASS.

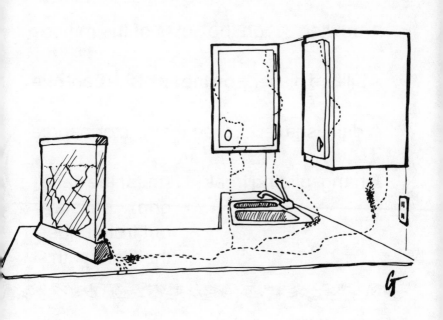

GREASY KIDS STUFF
or
SOME INTERESTING PLACES TO APPLY PETROLEUM JELLY

If your Ex happens to be:

A bowler .. on the soles of their shoes

A billiard player.. on the tip of the pool cue

A daily shaver ... on their razor handle

A hang-gliding freak... smear the hand-
grip. . .but stay
out from under
the flight path.

"On your Birthday,

I still think of all

those natural gifts

you'll never lose....

← FOLD →

WRINKLES!!

HAPPY BIRTHDAY, ACCORDIAN FACE!

Have a T-shirt made with the following words:

WILL ROGERS NEVER MET

(Your Ex's Name)

EX-HAUSTED

If your Ex is one of those eternally jealous types who, regardless of the way things are now, goes crazy at the mere thought of your being in another relationship, send a reasonable copy of the adjacent letter. It might make your Ex's day:

Dear *(Your Ex's Name):*

I don't know who else to turn to. I know you haven't heard from me in a while, but I wonder if I might ask you for some advice. It's about Lance/Chrissy of whom you may have heard. He's/She's a wonderful man/woman but has this sex problem. I tell you, *(Your Ex's Name),* Lance/Chrissy is an absolute **animal**.

Morning, noon and night, he's/she's after it constantly—not only does it in bed but in the bathtub, closet and garden.

He/She does it while I'm cooking—does it while I'm cleaning house—does it while I'm sorting laundry, doing dishes, for crying out loud!!

Thanks for listening.

Kindest Regards,

___(your name)___

P.S. Please forgive the shaky handwriting.

Bumper stickers are terrific because they can be used either way. That is, you can display a meaningful message on your own car or you can slap it on the rear bumper of your Ex's car the next time you happen to spot it outside a singles' bar. You know damn well your Ex is inside trying to get lucky. Chances are, the stickered bumper will never be noticed, since it's a medically proven fact that random lust clouds the vision. We think.

40

EX-PLANATIONS ♀

all your Ex's place. When the guy she's living
ith answers:

want to leave a message for Hungry Hips."

;he's not here right now."

know. But she'll be there in ten or fifteen
inutes. Ask her to check her car trunk, please.
hat's the third towel she's worn outta here this
eek."

tay up with current events. Has your Ex gone
nd gotten himself involved with somebody else
nd tried to wiggle out of that one, too? Help
pread the good news. ♂

all the newspapers and announce his en-
agement.

SON OF QUICKIES!

SWITCH THE LABELS BETWEEN YOUR EX'
AEROSOL CANS AND FEMININE SPRAY AN
DEODORANT.

IF YOUR EX INSISTS UPON KEEPING CUSTOD
OF THE WATERBED, GO AHEAD AND AGREE
THEN, ON THE DAY YOU MOVE OUT, PUMP I
FULL OF SLOW DRYING CEMENT.

DOES YOUR EX OWN A PARROT? TRAIN TH
BIRD SO THAT NO MATTER WHAT YOUR E
SAYS TO IT, THE PARROT SAYS "YOU BLEW
IT, TURKEY!"

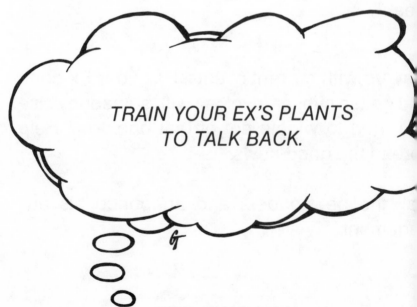

*TRAIN YOUR EX'S PLANTS
TO TALK BACK.*

ut algae food in your Ex's toilet bowl cleaner.
ur Ex will be tickled to death.

EX-CUSES, EX-CUSES

Nothing undermines a solid separation more quickly than for memories. They are not only counter-productive, but dangerou According to statistics, more separations fail because of tend thoughts than any other single destructive element.

At the first inkling of a melty thought, action must be swift ar decisive. Call your best friend. Have him remind you that:

- her lawyer can now afford that trip to Europe. With her.
- she washed your favorite pipe in low suds detergent.
- she thought it was cute to put K-Y jelly on your peanut butter sandwich.
- two can**not** live as cheaply as one.
- she used to slow down for green lights.
- she ate off your plate.
- you always had to conjure up fantasies because the real thing made you doze.
- she left hair in the sink.
- she kept everything in plastic bags, including your
  _____ .
  (fill in the blank)
- this is what you really wanted anyway.

These are only a few examples of typical female irrational behavior. Your Ex, of course, had her own particular brand of stupidity and distasteful acts. If you have trouble remembering the rest, your best friend won't. God knows, you've bitched about them long enough.

And for the other side there's always. . .

A LADY'S EXERCISE IN HATE

ere is an exercise designed to help you maintain the tensity of your dislike. For reinforcement, you can ompare yours with your fellow avengers.

'atching you shave used to make me _____.

'hen you and your mother were together, I could have st _____.

our friends made me _____.

our idea of a good time was to _____.

your underwear in the morning, you looked like a
_____.

your underwear at night, you looked like a tired
_____.

oing to a party with you was like going to a _____
_____ with a _____.

etting you to pick up the tab was like teaching a hippo
_____.

public, you have less class than _____.

private, you have less class than _____.

wished for a prince on a white charger, but instead I
ot a _____ on a _____.

though you're not very good at it, you can kiss my
_____ if you think I'll ever go through that again.

EX-ERCISE

Physical fitness is really good for you—especial
when your Ex does it. That way **you** don't get a
sweaty.

"How can I help out?" you wonder. Well. . .

- In case your Ex is a jogger, replace their ne
expensive, perfect-fitting jogging shoes with
duplicate pair—a couple of sizes smaller.

- Sign your Ex up for a midnight maratho
walking tour through high crime areas.

- If surfing is the current preferred form
exercise, give your Ex an all-day pass to th
local Wave Pool—and set the machine o
"TIDAL."

- Replace the strings on your Ex's favori
tennis racquet with piano wire—every time th
ball is hit, it'll be sliced like an orange.

*Replace a certain rubber racquetball with
a solid lead sphere. It won't do much for
your Ex's racquet, we admit, but think of
what could happen on the rebound. . .*

INHALE, EX-HALE

Adjust the numbers on your Ex's bathroom scale so that it appears they're losing weight, which will make them think they can eat everything in sight. In no time at all, your Ex will be the Queen or King of Flab City.

118 lbs.

You can ruin your Ex's day and (naturally) brighten up your own with a card expressing this tender philosophy:

"The only thing worse than *Loneliness*...

← FOLD →

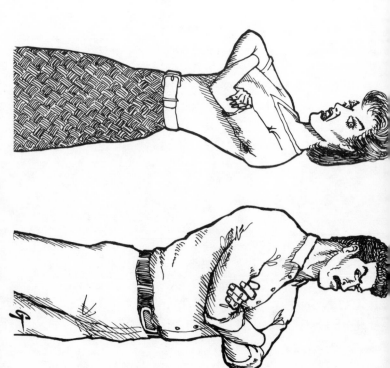

...is Togetherness with someone like you."

1-800...
TAKE-YOUR-PICK

kay, so your Ex got all the plastic. Turn that greedy maneuver around. Make it work in a positive, and positively nfuriating way. You already know—or can easily find out—he numbers on all those credit cards you both used to hare. Get them, get your telephone, get in front of the elevision set, and get busy.

emember, that's all those television salespeople need—he numbers. There's a wonderful world of weird products ght there at the tip of your dialing finger, and **doesn't your x need every one of them?** Besides, think about how nuch fun opening the mail will be when he or she starts etting the bills, for, say. . .

- EVERYBODY IN AMERICA'S GREATEST HITS!
- LIFETIME-GUARANTEED KNIFE SETS. . .
- KOREAN VETERANS' SUPPLEMENTARY INSUR-ANCE PLANS. . .
- SLICERS, PEELERS, GRINDERS, CHOPPERS, DICERS. . .
- EVERYBODY IN EUROPE'S GREATEST HITS!
- ALMOST-VALUABLE OBJECTS D'ART (Objects of art). . .
- WW-II VETERANS' SUPPLEMENTARY INSURANCE PLANS. . .
- EVERYBODY IN SOUTHEAST ASIA'S GREATEST HITS!
- TREES, SHRUBS, BUSHES, BULBS AND SEEDS. . .
- COINS, FLAGS AND STAMPS OF ALL NATIONS. . .
- EVERYBODY IN THE UNIVERSE'S GREATEST HITS!

FURTHER QUICKIES!

> ### SEND YOUR EX AN INVITATION TO A TRAIN WRECK.

Wanna ruin your Ex's next party? Show up.

HAVE PIZZA DELIVERED TO YOUR EX' WEIGHT WATCHER'S MEETING—EVERY TE MINUTES.

Reset each clock in your Ex's house fiv minutes apart. Don't forget their watch!

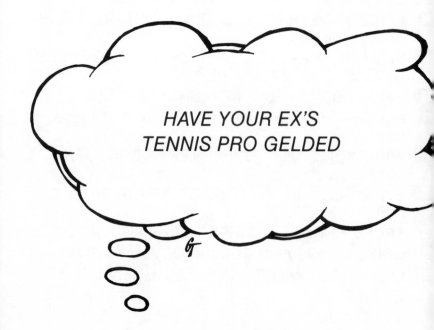

HAVE YOUR EX'S TENNIS PRO GELDED

What's this? Your Ex has just moved into the top floor of a high-rise condo? Okay, be a sport. Help out with the decorating. Order this special banner and have it hung across the inside of the picture window:

NO EX-PERIENCE NECESSARY

Call the place where your Ex is employed an
announce that you are the telegraph compar
operator with an important telegram.

Make sure it's written down so that they (an
curious co-workers) can't miss the message:

EASTERN UNION

CONGRATULATIONS—STOP—YOUR
APPLICATION TO KU KLUX KLAN
MEMBERSHIP ACCEPTED AND
APPROVED—STOP—SHEET TO
FOLLOW—STOP—

Sneak this onto the bumper of your Ex's car.
She'll have more action than a nymphomaniac
at a prison break.

EX-CHANGE GLANCES

Is your Ex part of a regular card playing club? On the day before the group meets at your Ex's place, go over and mark all the decks crudely. And then, in case the people your Ex plays with are too dumb, call up in the middle of the game and warn somebody!

GO TO THE AIRPORT AND HAND OUT NOTES. ON ONE SIDE WRITE, "PLEASE COME TO MY HOUSE AND BRING ALL THE MATERIAL YOU HAVE FOR SALE—I WOULD LIKE TO MAKE A GENEROUS DONATION." ON THE OTHER SIDE, YOUR EX'S NAME AND ADDRESS, AND "COME ANY TIME."

There is a device on the market today which is simply a microphone that will override the nearest FM radio. One night, while your Ex and a date are taking a romantic drive in the moonlight, interrupt the soft music with this urgent announcement:

"Your attention please, this is a public service alert. If any of our listeners know the whereabouts of (Your Ex's Name), please ask them to call the local Free Clinic immediately. Their drip test is back and it keeps eating its way through the lead container."

☞ **HO HUM** ☜

Every time you encounter one of your Ex's friends (if you can find any), yawn a lot (it should be easy with **those** friends). When they inquire about your apparently weary state, answer with some puzzlement:

"I can't understand why I'm so tired. . . after all, I went to bed **six** times last night!!!"

🔔

Help your Ex become part of the community. Call the appropriate number and volunteer your Ex's house for a meeting of Kleptomaniac's Anonymous. Do it just before Christmas.

You know those printed, annoying fliers you find flapping in the breeze under your windshield wipers in various parking lots? Usually you crumple and then toss them away, but we know you always read them first.

And so does everybody else.

So. Have some of your own fliers printed up announcing a meeting and pep rally at your Ex's house for the local chapter of the American Communist Party. Be sure you place a flier under every windshield wiper in the entire parking lot of your American Legion post. And don't forget the V.F.W.

EX-POSED

Save up all your empty booze bottles—make the rounds at all the local bars and gather all of theirs, too. Put them all in your Ex's trash cans on trash pick-up day when the cans are out front. **Then**, the neighbors will know you were telling the truth about what a big lush you had been putting up with.

OVER EX-POSED

Buy. . .

A) a bottle of hair color restorer
B) a jar of wrinkle cream
C) a large tube of hemorrhoid cream

Put them all in a transparent bag.

When you know your Ex is at lunch, say you're from the corner drug store when you deliver this stuff to your Ex's office.

"This," you tell your Ex's co-workers, "is an emergency delivery for one of our regular customers who's having another three-stage breakdown—ever since that weekend operation in Mexico. . ."

EX-ECUTIVE ERROR

Is your Ex in love with his or her car?

The next time your Ex is out of town, snatch and hide the precious thing—fabricate an insurance company letter notifying them that their policy (you have the number) is cancelled.

Then, along with the same "mail", the adjacent letter should arrive:

Dear (Your Ex's Name):

It is not without a blush of embarrassment and a tinge of regret that we inform you of a silly administrative error to wit:

Our new multi-million dollar Model B24-R City Trash Compactor (visitors welcome Wednesdays and Sundays) was accidentally misprogrammed. It has, as a result, ordered and effected the total destruction of several vehicles, including yours.

As a taxpaying citizen, you will certainly understand that our city is in no way legally liable for this sort of mishap. Rest assured, however, that to the best of our knowledge, it will never happen again.

Eunice Eichel

EUNICE EICHEL
City Clerk

A simple sentiment on a greeting card can go a
long way. As you know, little things affect little
minds. So, cut along the dotted line. Cut deep.
Pretend it's your Ex's heart. . .

"Despite the pain
and anguish,

I cannot forget the
time of our happiness

and love...

← FOLD →

1 minute, 33 seconds"

EX ANON

It is important that you join (form if necessary) a local EX ANON (EX'S ANONYMOUS) chapter so that you can call a clean single friend every time you get melty and want to give ol' What's his/her name one more chance.

In response to your desperate call, your EX ANON contact will hurry over and remind you:

- about the times your Ex developed sudden pains, migraines and compulsive interest in late-night television.

- of all the good cologne or aftershave you wasted on your Ex.

- about those historic moments when your Ex asked, "Was it good for you?" and you woke up long enough to nod, "yes."

- that your Ex believed a tuna and anchovy omelet before bedtime was an aphrodisiac.

- about the 'certain party' you thought was your best friend who wound up with $1,200 of **your** money.

- that your Ex still can't tell one simple joke, even after 726 futile attempts, which wasn't funny in the first place.

Thus reminded and re-strengthened, you're ready to get back to the serious business of even-getting.

PILLOW TALK

Something for your Ex to think about on his or her next visit to your house:

or, of course:

QUICKIES, ETC.

List your Ex's house with your Ex-realtor fo $12,500, nothing down and no payments unti the Federal Government balances the budget.

Got a cheapskate Ex-accountant who can't turr down a "Free Prize Gift?" Have a magnetic des pad delivered to his office and installed unde the master computer. **That** ought to clear a few floppy diskettes.

The sweet smell of successful Getting Even car be enjoyed by your Ex this winter. Leave ar anonymous gift. Nothing puts a snap in the ai like a roaring fire resting on rubber andirons Whew!

CALL THE PHONE COMPANY AND HAVE THEM INSTALL A PHONE WITH A DIFFERENT NUMBER IN EVERY ROOM OF YOUR EX'S HOUSE. THEN CALL THE COPS AND TELL THEM THERE'S A BOOKIE OPERATION AT THAT ADDRESS.

If your Ex lives in an apartment, first you have to buy one copy of "BLUEBOY," "GAY WORLD" or other magazines of the homosexual ilk, and one package of large address labels. Now:

A) Type his address clearly on the address label;

B) Peel off and affix the label in a prominent place on the magazine cover, making sure the title and content of the magazine remain obvious;

C) Leave the magazine on the floor in front of his apartment house mailbox, making sure its title and name are clearly displayed. For an added fillip, you can use a rubber stamp which says:

LIFETIME SUBSCRIBER

CAREER DAZE

Wait outside your Ex-doctor's office.

Every time somebody approaches, pretend you're just leaving and shout over your shoulder:

"Don't you **ever** clean your instruments?"

Every costume shop sells those head-caps which make you look bald. Buy one, put it on, get a folding chair and set it up outside your Ex-hairdresser's beauty shop. . . and sit there sobbing gently.

Follow your Ex-plumber's truck around town. Every time he leaves a job, knock at the door and announce that you're his bookkeeper. Say his tax bracket is too high, his conscience is bothering him, and he wants you to tell them to ignore his bill. This one's for free.

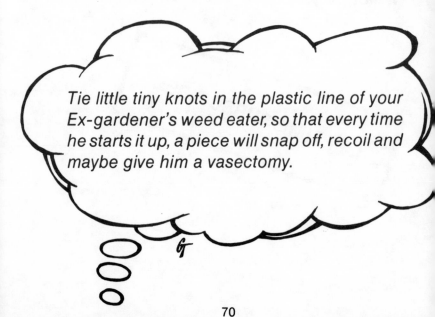

Tie little tiny knots in the plastic line of your Ex-gardener's weed eater, so that every time he starts it up, a piece will snap off, recoil and maybe give him a vasectomy.

WIRE YOUR EX-DENTIST'S ELECTRIC DRILL
INTO THE CALMING OFFICE MUSIC, TURN
UP THE VOLUME ALL THE WAY AND WATCH
THE WAITING ROOM CLEAR OUT!

Most attorneys don't advertise but you shou
let the world know your Ex-lawyer's specialty

Stick this on your Ex's bumper—after all it's yo
Ex-lawyer's specialty:

I'D RATHER BE LYING

ORIENTAL EX-PRESSIONS

Chinese food is not only good to eat, it's a great medium for messages and an even better way to communicate with your Ex's date on an anonymous basis. All you have to do is 1) type any or all of the following messages on a piece of paper and then cut them into appropriate-sized strips; 2) take a pair of tweezers and remove the dull, unimaginative fortunes from a plate of cookies and insert your own, and 3) make sure your Ex's companion receives them. Here are some suggestions:

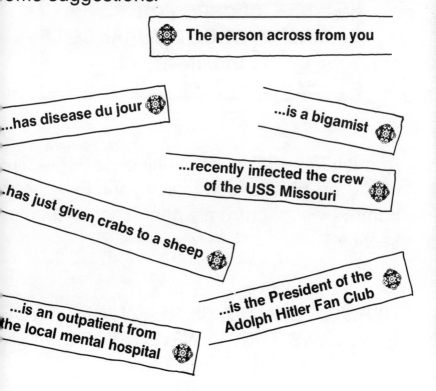

The person across from you

...has disease du jour

...is a bigamist

...recently infected the crew of the USS Missouri

...has just given crabs to a sheep

...is the President of the Adolph Hitler Fan Club

...is an outpatient from the local mental hospital

RETURN OF QUICKIES

Encourage a flock of local pigeons to mak
daily "runs" over your Ex's convertible. It shou
only take two or three loaves of bread until the
get the idea.

WHATEVER PROFESSION THEY'RE ENGAGE
IN, DON'T FORGET TO MOUNT THIS SIGN O
YOUR EX'S OFFICE DOOR:

> **CLOSED FOR**
> **MALPRACTICE INSURANCE**
> **SEMINAR**

And while we're on the subject of Better Bus
iness, be sure and register your Ex's phon
number with a currently popular sexual outca
service.

HERE'S A BEAUTY: BE REAL NICE TO YOU
EX IN-LAWS. THEY'LL *NEVER* STOP BLAMIN
YOUR EX FOR THE BREAKUP.

BUZZZZZZZZ...

s a scientific fact that flying insects such as ees, hornets and wasps are compulsively tracted to floral scents. So, be sure to spray ur Ex's doors, windows and rooms with some ally heavy, stinky, cheap air freshener.

Got nothing to do on a Saturday afternoon? When your Ex is out of the house or apartment, show your sympathetic, humane side by slipping into the house or apartment and cutting 'Emergency Exits' in all the roach hotels.

And yet another card for your Ex's special d

HAPPY BIRTHDAY!

By the way,
this is not a
Hallmark
card....

← FOLD →

...Because I don't care enough to send the very best!

LAST OF THE QUICKIES!

NEXT SUMMER, MIX SAND INTO YOUR EX'S SUNTAN LOTION; NEXT WINTER, DO THE SAME THING WITH YOUR EX'S LIP BALM.

Send your Ex a floral peace offering. . . Venus fly-traps aren't that expensive.

SHORT CIRCUIT YOUR EX'S VIBRATOR.

Turn the temperature control in your Ex's refrigerator to "off." That'll make the suppositories run together. Which is a better fit anyway.

IN YOUR EX'S NAME, ORDER SOME SEX TOYS FROM A CATALOG AND HAVE THEM SENT TO YOUR EX IN-LAWS.

Did your Ex just have some expensive land-
scaping done? Good. A thing of beauty should
be shared by all.

Organize a massive treasure hunt with a huge
cash prize. Have all the clues lead to digging up
your Ex's front and back yards and all the
flowerpots.

THE LAST WORD

Well, here we are. Feel better?

But if even this hasn't been enough, if you're still determined to do something to your Ex from which they'll never recover in this lifetime, we have one final, foolproof, never-miss, one hundred percent, 24-carat, drop-dead solution that is guaranteed to make sure your Ex will never, ever, *ever* forget you for the rest of his or her natural life. Here we go:

If you really want to Get Even With Your Ex. . .

GET BACK TOGETHER

ABOUT THE AUTHORS

MARSHA POSNER WILLIAMS is the Emmy
Award winning Producer of NBC'S "The Golden
Girls," and knows more dirty jokes than a
Masonic Lodge bartender. Despite the fact that
she has her own secretary, she can type 120
words a minute, but refuses to do so unless
bribed with Chinese food. She and Price have
been friends for so long that they don't even
bother lying to each other. Marsha is married to
Wayne Williams, top-flight Los Angeles photo-
grapher, who is much too smart for her.

MIKE PRICE is a motion picture/television/
magazine writer who thinks he knows everything
about everything. After a clumsy escape from
Hollywood, he moved to Bellevue (the town in
Tennessee, not the Manhattan hospital where
your Ex belongs!), which makes him the only non-
songwriter within hitchhiking distance of Nash-
ville. Price has brought seven legal marriages to
successful conclusion and is hopelessly enam-
ored of a lady known simply as "Boom-Boom
Annie," who is much too smart for him.

GET EVEN
&
GET PAID
COUPON

Send us your "Get Even With Your Ex" suggestion—real or fantasy—(use reverse side of this coupon). If we think it is funny or clever enough, your suggestions and your name will appear in one of our future books. Plus you will receive a $5.00 check and a complimentary copy of the book in which your suggestion appears.

Mail your submissions to:

    CCC Publications
    20306 Tau Place
    Chatsworth, CA 91311

Be sure to include your (legible) name and return address.

All submissions become the property of CCC Publications and cannot be returned.

YOUR "GET EVEN" SUGGESTION: _____

_____

_____

_____

_____

_____

_____

_____

_____

_____

_____

_____

_____

_____

_____

YOUR NAME & ADDRESS: _____

_____

_____

_____